C000065444

THIS BOOK BELONGS TO...

Name:	Age:

Favourite player:

2022/2023

My Predictions...	Actual...

The Rams' final position:

The Rams' top scorer:

League One winners:

League One top scorer:

FA Cup winners:

EFL Cup winners:

EFL Trophy winners:

Contributors: Luke Ingram, Mark Lawrence, Tom Loakes, Peter Rogers, Andy Greeves.

A TWOCAN PUBLICATION

©2022. Published by twocan under licence from Derby County Football Club.

ISBN: 978-1-914588-71-6

£9

CONTENTS

GOAL
OF THE
SEASON

KRYSTIAN BIELIK VS BIRMINGHAM CITY

Hollywood would have been proud of this story. A real comeback tale and a defining moment in the career of Krystian Bielik and Derby County. And not just because his acrobatic overhead-kick against Birmingham City won the club's Goal of the Season, but the significance of the strike will live long in the memory of the Derby faithful.

Picture the scene, 33,000 Derby supporters marching in unison to Pride Park Stadium before the game to show their undoubted love for their club. Banners, flags and chants drowned out the feeling of anguish and adversity, following threats of liquidation. It was a defiant atmosphere.

But on the pitch, Derby struggled to get going. Lyle Taylor put the Blues ahead, before Scott Hogan doubled their lead just after the half-time interval. Derby needed a spark and turned to their bench for inspiration. Step up Krystian Bielik.

After suffering two career-threatening knee injuries, the second of which was suffered exactly twelve months to the day before this match, Krystian's strike began to change Derby's fortunes. With fans losing hope that anything could be salvaged from the game, Luke Plange pulled a goal back with only minutes on the clock.

It sparked a frantic finale. Bodies were thrown forward as the Rams laid siege to the Blues' box, and then in the 95th minute, redemption. Bielik, after all of his battles with injury, almost lifted the roof off Pride Park when his bicycle-kick hit the top corner of the net. Elation.

Only one point may have been won, but the goal signified much more than that. It renewed faith and optimism, and for a split second, everything was forgotten. An incredible moment!

KRYSTIAN
BIELIK

RUNNERS-UP

RAVEL MORRISON VS BARNSLEY

If you were to define a team goal, just show them Ravel Morrison's opening strike in the 2-0 victory over Barnsley in March 2022.

One touch passing, good movement off the ball and a delightfully dinked finish. The video earned 3.1 million views on Twitter. Unfortunate to miss out on the top prize.

TOM LAWRENCE VS SHEFFIELD UNITED (FIRST GOAL)

A piece of individual brilliance for Derby's 2021/22 captain Tom Lawrence earned a valuable three points against promotion-hopefuls Sheffield United at Pride Park Stadium in January 2022.

The Welshman picked up the ball, waltzed past one player, dragged it around another before firing into the bottom corner to lift the roof off Pride Park Stadium, before scoring a superb second soon afterwards to round off a 2-0 victory.

NUMBER OF SEASONS WITH THE RAMS:

6

DERBY COUNTY LEAGUE APPEARANCES:

227

DERBY COUNTY LEAGUE GOALS:

68

PLAYER OF THE SEASON WINNER:

1992/93

LEGEND

MARCO GABBIADINI

DERBY COUNTY ACHIEVEMENTS:

First Division runners-up 1995/96
Anglo-Italian Cup runners-up 1992/93

MAJOR STRENGTH:

Beating defenders for pace and skill,
before beating the goalkeeper with power

INTERNATIONAL ACTION:

Also eligible to represent Italy,
Gabbiadini played twice for the
England U21s and once for England 'B',
but never for the senior team

FINEST HOUR:

Gabbiadini was named Derby
Player of the Season in his first
full campaign at the club

What do Marco Gabbiadini and Chris Martin have in common? Firstly, they were both excellent strikers!

And secondly, they both enjoyed journeyman careers but stayed at Derby County longer than anywhere else. Between the two of them, they hit the back of the net 146 times for the club...

...But which Rams legend was better?

NUMBER OF SEASONS
WITH THE RAMS:

8

DERBY COUNTY
LEAGUE APPEARANCES:

238

DERBY COUNTY LEAGUE GOALS:

78

PLAYER OF THE SEASON WINNER:

Never

LEGEND

CHRIS MARTIN

DERBY COUNTY ACHIEVEMENTS:

Championship Play-Offs runners-up
2013/14
Championship Play-Offs semi-finalists
2015/16

MAJOR STRENGTH:

Martin's shot power
was outrageous

INTERNATIONAL ACTION:

Despite playing and scoring for England
U19s, Martin has 17 Scotland caps,
with his father having been born in Glasgow

FINEST HOUR:

Scoring against Brighton & Hove
Albion in the 2013/14 Championship
Play-Off semi-final first leg

33

CURTIS
DAVIES

Defending is not just about stopping the attackers and clearing your lines. Making the best of possession you have just won is vital - although the danger has to be cleared, it is important for your team to keep hold of the ball.

SOCCER
SKILLS
LONG PASSES

When passing your way out of defence, and short, side-foot passes are not possible, the longer pass, driven over the heads of midfield players, can be used.

EXERCISE

In an area 40m x 10m, A1 and A2 try to pass accurately to each other, with a defender B, in the middle between them. Player B must attempt to stop the pass if possible, and A1 and A2, must keep the ball within the area of the grids.

After each successful long pass, the end player will exchange a shorter pass with B before passing long again, thus keeping the exercise realistic and also keeping the defender in the middle involved. The player in the middle should be changed every few minutes, and a 'count' of successful passes made for each player.

KEY FACTORS

1　Approach at an angle.
2　Non kicking foot placed next to the ball.
3　Eye on the ball.
4　Strike underneath the ball & follow through.

Practice is the key to striking a consistently accurate long pass and to developing the timing and power required.

The same end result could be achieved by bending the pass around the defender instead of over him, and this pass could be practised in the same exercise, by striking the football on its outer edge (instead of underneath) which will impart the spin required to make the ball 'bend' around the defender - not an easy skill!

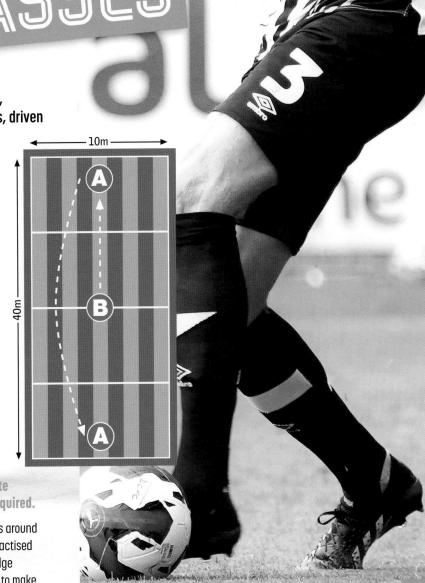

11

LEAGUE ONE
2022/2023
SQUAD

1

JOE WILDSMITH

GOALKEEPER   DOB: 28/12/1995   COUNTRY: ENGLAND

Joe Wildsmith ended his 14-year association with Sheffield Wednesday in the summer of 2022 as he elected to join Derby County, signing a two-year contract. The shot-stopper was immediately handed the number one shirt and kept a clean sheet on his debut as the Rams beat Oxford United on the opening day of the 2022/23 Sky Bet League One campaign.

3 CRAIG FORSYTH

LEFT BACK DOB: 24/02/1989 COUNTRY: SCOTLAND

The 2022/23 campaign is a huge milestone for Craig Forsyth who celebrates his tenth season with Derby County Football Club. The Scottish defender, who has made more than 250 appearances for the club, is the squad's longest-serving player and a favourite amongst Rams' supporters. He is solid in defence and offers a threat going forward, scoring three goals during the 2021/22 campaign.

4 CONOR HOURIHANE

MIDFIELD DOB: 02/02/1991 COUNTRY: ROI

An experienced midfielder with proven quality in the higher divisions, Conor Hourihane chose to join Derby County in the summer of 2022 as part of the club's rebuild following the successful takeover of the club by Clowes Developments (UK) Ltd. The Republic of Ireland international made an immediate impact, scoring on his debut in a 1-0 victory over Oxford United.

5

JAMES CHESTER

DEFENDER DOB: 23/01/1989 COUNTRY: WALES

James Chester put pen-to-paper on a one-year contract with Derby County in the 2022 summer transfer window and offers valuable experience to the defensive back-line. Goalscorer in the 2014 FA Cup final for Hull City against Arsenal, it's the first time Chester has dropped into League One permanently after playing the majority of his career between the Premier League and Championship.

6

EIRAN CASHIN

DEFENDER DOB: 09/11/2001 COUNTRY: ROI

A product of the Derby County Academy, Eiran Cashin made his breakthrough into the Derby County first team at the end of the 2021/22 campaign. The no-nonsense defender made 18 appearances in total and even scored his first goal in a Rams' shirt in a 2-0 victory over Blackpool at Bloomfield Road, heading home from a Malcolm Ebiowei free kick.

LEAGUE ONE
2022/2023
SQUAD

7

TOM
BARKHUIZEN

FORWARD   DOB: 04/07/1993   COUNTRY: ENGLAND

Tom Barkhuizen's move to Derby County is the first time he has ventured away from the North West on a permanent basis after the forward signed a two-year contract with the Rams in the summer of 2022. The 29-year-old has spent time with Blackpool, Morecambe and Preston North End, where he has spent the last five-and-a-half years, but swapped Deepdale for the East Midlands.

8 MAX BIRD 8
MIDFIELDER DOB: 18/09/2000 COUNTRY: ENGLAND

A promising Academy graduate, Max Bird was named vice-captain of Derby County ahead of the 2022/23 Sky Bet League One campaign. Now in his sixth season around the first-team environment, the midfielder has accrued more than 100 appearances in a Rams' shirt and scored his first goal for the club last season on his 21st birthday in a 2-1 victory over Stoke City.

9 JAMES COLLINS
FORWARD DOB: 01/12/1990 COUNTRY: ROI

James Collins arrived at Pride Park Stadium with a reputation for scoring goals and with several promotions on his impressive CV. The striker, who has earned international recognition with the Republic of Ireland, boasts more than 175 career goals to his name and has enjoyed promotions with Shrewsbury Town, Northampton Town and Luton Town over the past ten years.

LEAGUE ONE
2022/2023
SQUAD

10
DAVID McGOLDRICK

FORWARD DOB: 29/11/1987 COUNTRY: ROI

Playing in the Premier League two seasons ago with Sheffield United, David McGoldrick adds quality to the attacking areas at Pride Park Stadium. Hailing from nearby Nottingham, the striker has over 500 career appearances to his name, scoring more than 125 goals. An all-round team player, his technical ability sets him apart from other forwards in the division.

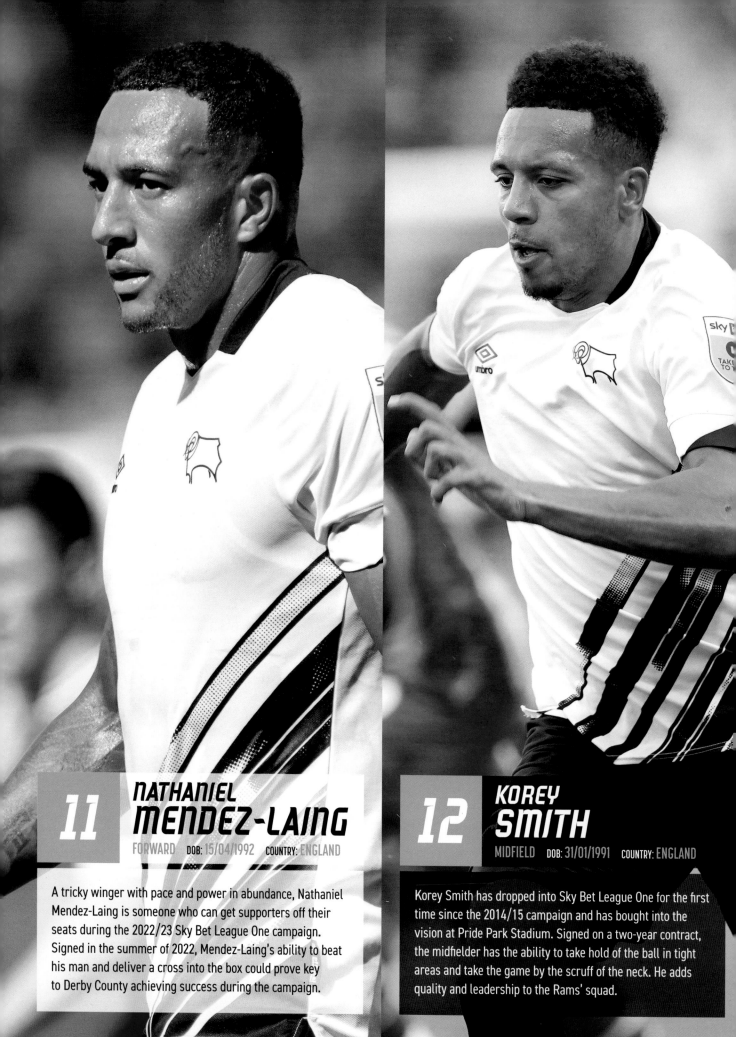

11 NATHANIEL MENDEZ-LAING

FORWARD DOB: 15/04/1992 COUNTRY: ENGLAND

A tricky winger with pace and power in abundance, Nathaniel Mendez-Laing is someone who can get supporters off their seats during the 2022/23 Sky Bet League One campaign. Signed in the summer of 2022, Mendez-Laing's ability to beat his man and deliver a cross into the box could prove key to Derby County achieving success during the campaign.

12 KOREY SMITH

MIDFIELD DOB: 31/01/1991 COUNTRY: ENGLAND

Korey Smith has dropped into Sky Bet League One for the first time since the 2014/15 campaign and has bought into the vision at Pride Park Stadium. Signed on a two-year contract, the midfielder has the ability to take hold of the ball in tight areas and take the game by the scruff of the neck. He adds quality and leadership to the Rams' squad.

LEAGUE ONE
2022/2023
SQUAD

15 HAYDON ROBERTS

DEFENDER · DOB: 10/05/2002 · COUNTRY: ENGLAND

A promising defender with bundles of talent, Haydon Roberts has a bright future in the game. Signed on a season-long loan deal from Brighton & Hove Albion, the defender, who has been capped at England youth levels, is hoping his stay with the Rams will aid his development both personally and professionally. Roberts can play at both left-back and centre-half.

16 LIAM **THOMPSON**

MIDFIELDER DOB: 29/04/2002 COUNTRY: ENGLAND

Liam Thompson earned huge praise following his breakthrough season with Derby County during the 2021/22 campaign. He made his debut against AFC Bournemouth at Pride Park Stadium in November 2021 and put in a man-of-the-match display in a 3-2 victory, whilst he went on to make 24 appearances in all competitions. His new contract which was signed in July 2022 takes him to the end of the 2023/24 campaign.

17 LOUIE **SIBLEY**

MIDFIELDER DOB: 13/09/2001 COUNTRY: ENGLAND

Nobody will forget Louie Sibley's introduction to the first-team environment at Derby County. He scored a wonder strike on his full league debut in March 2020 as the Rams ran out 3-0 winners over Blackburn Rovers at Pride Park. Now in his third full season as a professional, Sibley will be aiming to fulfil his undoubted quality this campaign.

LEAGUE ONE
2022/2023
SQUAD

18 LEWIS DOBBIN

FORWARD · **DOB:** 03/01/2003 · **COUNTRY:** ENGLAND

Lewis Dobbin arrived at Pride Park Stadium on a season-long loan deal from Everton in August 2022. He has already made his Toffees debut, playing five times in all competitions. He came off the bench against Manchester United and Chelsea as Everton drew both games 1-1. With pace and an eye for a finish, Dobbin adds an extra option to Derby's impressive attacking line.

19 RICHARD **STEARMAN**

DEFENDER   DOB: 19/08/1987   COUNTRY: ENGLAND

A leader both on and off the pitch, defender Richard Stearman put pen-to-paper on a new one-year contract with Derby County in the summer of 2022. The former Leicester City, Wolverhampton Wanderers and Sheffield United centre-half has amassed more than 500 appearances in the game and adds valuable experience to the younger players within the Rams' squad.

21 SCOTT LOACH

GOALKEEPER DOB: 27/05/1988 COUNTRY: ENGLAND

Goalkeeper Scott Loach arrived at Pride Park Stadium in the summer of 2022 from neighbours Chesterfield where he made 48 appearances as they reached the National League Play-Offs last season. Signed to support the Rams' other senior goalkeepers and pass on his knowledge and expertise, Loach has a huge role to play for Derby this season after signing a one-year contract.

30 KWAKU ODUROH

DEFENDER DOB: 16/10/2002 COUNTRY: ENGLAND

Kwaku Oduroh joined Derby County in July 2022 after leaving Manchester City where he had been for more than a decade. Initially on trial, the right-back excelled in a pre-season friendly victory over Bradford City and earned himself a two-year contract with the Rams. Oduroh captained City's U18s side during the 2020/21 campaign and he also spent time with Tottenham Hotspur last season.

23 WILLIAM OSULA

FORWARD DOB: 04/08/2003 COUNTRY: DENMARK

Derby County completed the Transfer Deadline Day signing of promising Sheffield United forward William Osula on a season-long loan in September 2022. Originally on the youth books of FC Copenhagen in Denmark, he joined Sheffield United in 2018 and signed professional terms in the summer of 2021, making his first-team debut came as a sub for the Blades in a 0-0 draw at Blackpool in March 2022. He made his first appearance for Denmark at youth level when he featured for their U19s in a friendly against Hungary in early 2022.

32 JOSEPH ANANG

GOALKEEPER DOB: 08/06/2000 COUNTRY: ENGLAND

Goalkeeper Joseph Anang joined Derby County on a season-long loan from Premier League West Ham United in August 2022. Born in Ghana, Anang moved to England in his younger years and joined the Hammers' youth system as a scholar in 2017. He made their first-team bench as an unused sub at Crystal Palace December 2019, just weeks after making his England U20s debut in a 3-0 win over Iceland. After loan spells with Stevenage and League of Ireland Premier Division side St Patrick's Athletic, he returned to West Ham in order to link up with the Rams.

33 CURTIS DAVIES

DEFENDER DOB: 15/03/1985 COUNTRY: ENGLAND

Curtis Davies enters his sixth full season with Derby County after experiencing one his best in professional football. The defender played every minute of every game during the 2021/22 campaign and was voted the club's Jack Stamps Player of the Season for his impressive displays. The defender has been handed the captaincy ahead of the new 2022/23 campaign.

LEAGUE ONE
2022/2023
SQUAD

34 JAKE ROONEY
DEFENDER   DOB: 22/08/2003   COUNTRY: ENGLAND

The cousin of former Derby manager and player Wayne Rooney, Jake Rooney joined Derby County on a permanent basis in August 2022 after a trial period, making his senior debut in a 2-1 round one victory at Mansfield Town in the Carabao Cup. Having progressed through the Burnley youth ranks after joining the Clarets at the age of 14, he was named as their Youth Team Player of the Year for the 2020/21 campaign and he kicked on to establish himself in their Premier League 2 side.

38 JASON KNIGHT
MIDFIELDER   DOB: 13/02/2001   COUNTRY: ROI

An Academy product with bundles of energy and potential, Jason Knight's versatility is what makes him so valuable to Derby's squad. Able to play at right-back, in centre-midfield or out wide, Knight shines regardless of his position. Capped by the Republic of Ireland national team, the midfielder passed 100 appearances for Derby during the 2021/22 campaign.

Here are ten Multiple Choice questions to challenge your footy knowledge!

Good luck...

MULTIPLE
CHOICE

ANSWERS ON PAGE 62

1. What was the name of Tottenham Hotspur's former ground?

A) White Rose Park
B) White Foot Way
C) White Hart Lane

2. Which club did Steven Gerrard leave to become Aston Villa manager?

A) Liverpool,
B) Glasgow Rangers
C) LA Galaxy

3. Mohamed Salah and Son Heung-min were joint winners of the Premier League Golden Boot as the division's top scorers in 2021/22.

How many goals did they score?

A) 23   B) 24   C) 25

4. What is the nationality of Manchester United boss Erik ten Hag?

A) Swiss   B) Dutch
C) Swedish

5. Where do Everton play their home games?

A) Goodison Road
B) Goodison Way
C) Goodison Park

6. From which club did Arsenal sign goalkeeper Aaron Ramsdale?

A) Sheffield United
B) Stoke City
C) AFC Bournemouth

7. What is Raheem Sterling's middle name?

A) Shaun
B) Shaquille
C) Silver

8. Who won the 2021/22 League One Play-Off final?

A) Wigan Athletic
B) Sunderland
C) Rotherham United

9. How many Championship goals did Matej Vydra score for the Rams when he won the division's Golden Boot award in 2017/18?

A) 21   B) 22   C) 23

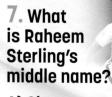

10. Which club was Korey Smith last contracted to before joining the Rams in the summer of 2022?

A) Bristol City
B) Norwich City
C) Swansea City

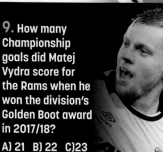

26

8

MAX
BIRD

ANSWERS ON PAGE 62

CLASSIC FAN'TASTIC

Rammie is hiding in the crowd in five different places as Derby County fans celebrate being crowned First Division champions in 1975. Can you find all five?

DAVE MACKAY

COLIN TODD

BRUCE RIOCH

ROD THOMAS

6

EIRAN CASHIN

Close control in tight situations creates havoc in opposition defences - particularly when receiving the ball in the air - and nine times out of ten, when a striker receives the ball, he has his back to goal.

SOCCER
SKILLS
RECEIVING THE BALL

Quite often the ball will arrive in the air, and good strikers have to be able to cope with that - controlling and turning in one movement, ready for the instant shot.

EXERCISE 1

In an area 20m x 10m, two players A and A2 test the man in the middle, B, by initially throwing the ball at him in the air, with the instruction to turn and play in to the end man - if possible using only two touches.

The middle player is changed regularly, and to make things more realistic, the end players progress to chipping the ball into the middle.

The middle player is asked to receive and turn using chest, thigh, or instep.

KEY FACTORS

1   Assess flight early - get in position.
2   Cushion the ball.
3   Be half turned as you receive.

EXERCISE 2

A progression of this exercise is the following, where the ball is chipped or driven in to the striker from varying positions. He has to receive with his back to goal, and using just two touches in total if possible, shoot past the keeper into the goal!

To make this even more difficult, a defender can be brought in eventually. For younger children, the 'servers' should throw the ball to ensure consistent quality.

TRAIN TO WIN

Making sure that you are fit, healthy and fully prepared is key to success in whatever challenge you are taking on. Those three factors are certainly vital for professional footballers and also for any young aspiring player who plays for his or her school or local football team. The importance of fitness, health and preparation are key factors behind the work that goes into preparing the Derby County players to perform at their maximum on matchday.

The Rams players will need to demonstrate peak levels of fitness if they want to feature in Liam Rosenior's team. Before anyone can think of pulling on a smart white shirt and stepping out at Pride Park, they will have had to perform well at the Training Ground to have shown the manager, his coaches and fitness staff that they are fully fit and ready for the physical challenges that await them on a matchday.

Regardless of whether training takes place at the training ground or at the stadium, the players' fitness remains an all-important factor. Of course time spent practicing training drills and playing small-sided games will help a player's fitness but there is lots of work undertaken just to ensure maximum levels of fitness are reached.

Away from the training pitches the players will spend a great deal of time in the gymnasium partaking in their own personal work-outs. Bikes, treadmills and weights will all form part of helping the players reach and maintain a top level of fitness.

Over the course of a week the players will take part in many warm-up and aerobic sessions and even complete yoga and pilates classes to help with core strength and general fitness. The strength and conditioning coaches at the club work tirelessly to do all they can to make sure that the players you see in action are at their physical peak come kick-off.

While the manager and his staff will select the team and agree the tactics, analysts will provide the players and staff with details on the opposition's strengths, weaknesses and their likely approach to the match.

Suffice to say the training ground is a busy place and no stone is left unturned in preparation for the big match!

PLAYER

OF THE

SEASON

If you want one player in the trenches with you, Curtis Davies would probably top your list. He is a leader, wears his heart on his sleeve and is a true professional to the game of football. Rightfully, he was voted as Derby County's 2021/22 Jack Stamps Player of the Season, but his story starts prior to the last game of the previous campaign.

Because when leaders are needed, they step up. With Derby needing at least a point to retain their Championship status, he showed incredible courage and resilience, defying medical advice to be named on the substitute's bench. Less than five months previous, he had suffered a serious Achilles injury.

He shouldn't have been there. He wasn't fit, he hadn't trained and the chances of causing another serious injury was high, but he was determined. He donned the shirt, played the final ten minutes and came through the closing stages of the thrilling 3-3 draw against Sheffield Wednesday unscathed as Derby's immediate on-field future was secured.

Off-field adversity followed, but Davies once again led with his chest out in his performances on the pitch and his pleas off it. He had arguably his best season in a Derby shirt, looking composed and assured in a role slightly unfamiliar with what he is used to.

He went on to play every minute of every league game, scoring three goals which included a bullet header in the dying minutes against Reading in January 2022 to earn a 2-2 draw.

An inspiration to many and a true leader of our football club, he deservedly won the award.

CURTIS
DAVIES

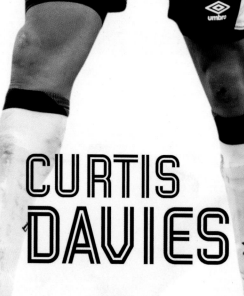

YOUNG PLAYER OF THE SEASON

Max Bird claimed the 2021/22 Sammy Crooks Young Player of the Season award following another impressive campaign for Derby County. It's the second time Bird has won the award following his 2019/20 success.

The Academy graduate, who made his debut at the age of 16 in an EFL Cup tie against Barnsley in August 2017, enjoyed another fruitful season, scoring two goals in 43 appearances.

He marked his 21st birthday in September 2021 with his first professional goal, a corker from 25-yards into the top corner in an emotionally-charged victory over Stoke City, whilst he surpassed 100 appearances in a 3-1 victory over Hull City in February 2022.

DREAM TEAM

Pick your ultimate Derby County dream team and design them a kit!

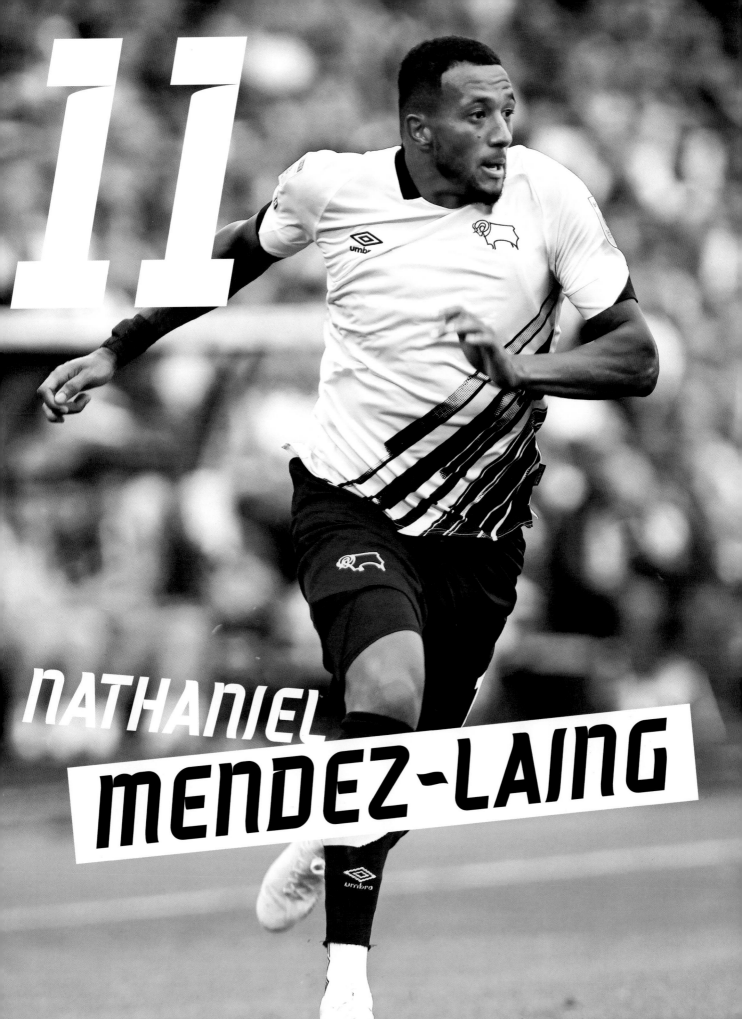

11

NATHANIEL
MENDEZ-LAING

ACCRINGTON STANLEY
SEAN McCONVILLE

With approaching 300 career appearances across two spells with the club, midfielder Sean McConville is a true Accrington Stanley legend.

A reliable performer and probably the first name on manager John Coleman's team-sheet, Sean has played a great part in helping Stanley secure a fourth consecutive season at League One level.

LEAGUE ONE
DANGER MEN

THE OFFICIAL 2023 DERBY COUNTY ANNUAL TAKES A LOOK AT 24 LEAGUE ONE STARS THAT COULD PERFORM VITAL ROLES FOR THEIR CLUBS DURING THE 2022/23 SEASON.

BARNSLEY
DEVANTE COLE

The son of former Newcastle United, Manchester United and England striker Andy Cole, 27-year-old Devante Cole is now in his second spell with the Tykes having previously played on loan at Oakwell in 2014/15.

The striker netted five goals in 19 appearances when on loan from Manchester City and will be looking to establish a formidable partnership with new signing James Norwood at League One level in 2022/23.

BRISTOL ROVERS
JOHN MARQUIS

Following their dramatic final-day promotion to the third tier last season, Bristol Rovers completed the signing of expert League One marksman John Marquis.

A prolific goalscorer with Doncaster Rovers and Portsmouth, Marquis joined Rovers following a short-term deal with Lincoln City. With the ability to cause problems for defenders in the air or on the ground - his first Bristol Rovers goal secured a 1-0 victory over Oxford United earlier this season.

BOLTON WANDERERS
ELIAS KACHUNGA

A mobile and intelligent forward, Elias Kachunga made his mark in the UK with Huddersfield Town as the Terriers won promotion to the Premier League in 2016/17.

A full Congolese international, Kachunga joined Bolton from Sheffield Wednesday in 2021. Now in his second season at the club, the 30-year-old forward will have a key role to play over the coming months.

BURTON ALBION
DAVIS KEILLOR-DUNN

Burton Albion snapped up goalscoring midfielder Davis from Oldham Athletic in the summer of 2022 following the Boundary Park club's fall to the National League.

The 24-year-old midfielder scored 28 goals from midfield across two seasons with the Latics and opened his Albion account with a hat-trick in the opening month of the 2022/23 League One season as the Brewers drew 4-4 away to Accrington Stanley.

CAMBRIDGE UNITED
JOE IRONSIDE

Cambridge United striker Joe Ironside scored 15 goals last season, including a historic strike in Cambridge's shock 1-0 FA Cup victory over Premier League giants Newcastle United at St James' Park in January 2022.

The 29-year-old striker also bagged a hat-trick in the 5-0 League One win away to Cheltenham Town. Ironside is expected to be the team's main goal threat again in 2022/23.

DERBY COUNTY
DAVID McGOLDRICK

Derby County secured the signing of former Republic of Ireland international striker David McGoldrick in July 2022.

The arrival of such an experienced and proven goalscorer is sure to boost the Rams for their 2022/23 League One campaign. A skilful and intelligent forward, McGoldrick has great ability to link-up play in the final third and score goals too.

CHARLTON ATHLETIC
JAYDEN STOCKLEY

Former Preston North End striker Jayden Stockley moved to Charlton Athletic in the summer of 2021 having spent the previous six months on loan at The Valley.

He reached double figures in League One last season with 13 goals and netted his first of 2022/23 in the Addicks' 5-1 demolition of Plymouth Argyle in August 2022.

EXETER CITY
MATT JAY

Another young player to have emerged from the Exeter City Academy, midfielder Matt Jay contributed a whopping 14 goals from midfield as the Grecians won promotion from League Two last season.

The most significant of his goals came in April 2022 as Barrow were defeated 2-1 with Jay netting the winning goal that secured promotion. A very highly rated performer, Jay will be keen to prove his worth at League One Level this season.

CHELTENHAM TOWN
ALFIE MAY

Striker Alfie May enjoyed a 26-goal season for Cheltenham Town in 2021/22 when his goals proved vital in the club maintaining League One status.

Of his 26 goals last season, 23 came in League One including a brace against former club Doncaster Rovers in a 4-0 victory - while in February 2022 he scored four goals in an amazing 5-5 draw with Wycombe Wanderers at Adams Park.

FLEETWOOD TOWN
HARVEY MACADAM

Plucked from National League North side Ashton United in the January 2022 transfer window, 21-year-old midfielder Harvey Macadam marked his full league debut with a goal in the Cod Army's 3-1 win at Crewe in April 2022.

Macadam will be out to impress new Fleetwood boss Scott Brown this season as he aims to make a first-team place his own in 2022/23.

FOREST GREEN ROVERS
JAMILLE MATT

Striker Jamille Matt netted 20 goals in all competitions last season as Forest Green Rovers won the League Two title and sealed a first promotion to the third tier.

The Jamaican front-man will form the focal point of the attack at the New Lawn in 2022/23 as Forest Green attempt to establish themselves at League One level.

MK DONS
BRADLEY JOHNSON

A vastly-experienced central midfielder, Bradley Johnson joined MK Dons in the summer of 2022.

His knowledge and knowhow are sure to be of great benefit to the younger players in the Dons' squad and the 35-year-old showed his new fans he still knows where the goal is as he scored twice to give Liam Manning's team their first win of the season when they defeated Port Vale in August.

IPSWICH TOWN
MARCUS HARNESS

Ipswich Town swooped on League One rivals Portsmouth for the services of goalscoring midfielder Marcus Harness in July 2022.

A very skilful and pacy winger, Harness can operate on either flank and his versatility is sure to be of great benefit to Kieran McKenna's side as they plan their 2022/23 League One campaign and push for automatic promotion to the Championship.

MORECAMBE
JONATHAN OBIKA

A product of the Tottenham Hotspur Academy, striker Jonathan Obika was capped by England at both U19 and U20 level earlier in his career.

Obika joined Morecambe from St Mirren in June 2021 and his twelve appearances and two goals helped the Shrimpers maintain their third tier status last season. The 32-year-old will be keen for more games and goals in the current campaign.

OXFORD UNITED
JOSH MURPHY

A former FA Youth Cup winner and Premier League star with Norwich City and Cardiff City, winger Josh Murphy brings experience, pace and a real goal threat to the Oxford United League One promotion push.

A player capable of producing the spectacular, Murphy's arrival at the Kassam Stadium has been seen as a great coup for Oxford United.

LINCOLN CITY
TOM HOPPER

Forward Tom Hopper was handed the Lincoln City captaincy for the 2022/23 season by new boss Mark Kennedy.

A regular goalscorer at Sincil Bank since joining the Imps from Southend United in January 2020, Hopper started the current campaign in fine form with an opening-day goal against Exeter City and was then on target in Lincoln's 2-1 win at Oxford.

PETERBOROUGH UNITED
JONSON CLARKE-HARRIS

Proven League One marksman Jonson Clarke-Harris fired home 31 league goals in Posh's 2020/21 promotion-winning campaign.

His dozen Championship goals could not help United avoid the drop last season, but his form in front of goal will certainly prove vital to any success the London Road club enjoys.

PLYMOUTH ARGYLE
FINN AZAZ

Plymouth Argyle boosted their firepower for the 2022/23 League One campaign with the loan signing of highly-rated Aston Villa youngster Finn Azaz.

The 22-year-old attacking midfielder was on target three times in the opening month of the season for an Argyle side that harbour ambitions of at least a Play-Off place come the end of the campaign.

SHEFFIELD WEDNESDAY
MICHAEL SMITH

A summer signing from South Yorkshire rivals Rotherham United, striker Michael Smith is something of a League One promotion specialist having secured a hat-trick of promotions to the second tier while at the New York Stadium.

A prolific scorer at this level, Smith netted 25 goals in all competitions for the Millers last season and the Hillsborough faithful will be hopeful of a similar return in 2022/23.

PORT VALE
ELLIS HARRISON

Much-travelled centre-forward Ellis Harrison reunited with his former Bristol Rovers manager Darrell Clarke when he joined Port Vale at the start of the new 2022/23 season.

Harrison has great physical attributes and is an excellent League One target man - he netted his first Vale goals in back-to-back games against MK Dons and Burton Albion in August 2022.

SHREWSBURY TOWN
JORDAN SHIPLEY

Former Republic of Ireland U21 international Jordan Shipley joined Shrewsbury Town in May 2022.

The 25-year-old goalscoring midfielder was signed from Coventry City and with vast Championship experience, Shipley is expected to be a key performer for the Shrews in League One this season. He netted his first goal for his new club in their 2-0 win at Forest Green in September 2022.

PORTSMOUTH
COLBY BISHOP

Recruited from League One rivals Accrington Stanley in July 2022, forward Colby Bishop has made a flying start to his Fratton Park career.

The 25-year-old netted a highly impressive five goals in his first five outings in a Portsmouth shirt including both goals in a 2-0 victory away to Cheltenham Town.

WYCOMBE WANDERERS
SAM VOKES

Former Wales international forward Sam Vokes brings power, strength and a wealth of experience to the Wycombe attack.

The 32-year-old scored 17 League One goals last season as Chairboys' campaign to return to the Championship saw them reach the League One Play-Off final where they lost 2-0 to Sunderland at Wembley.

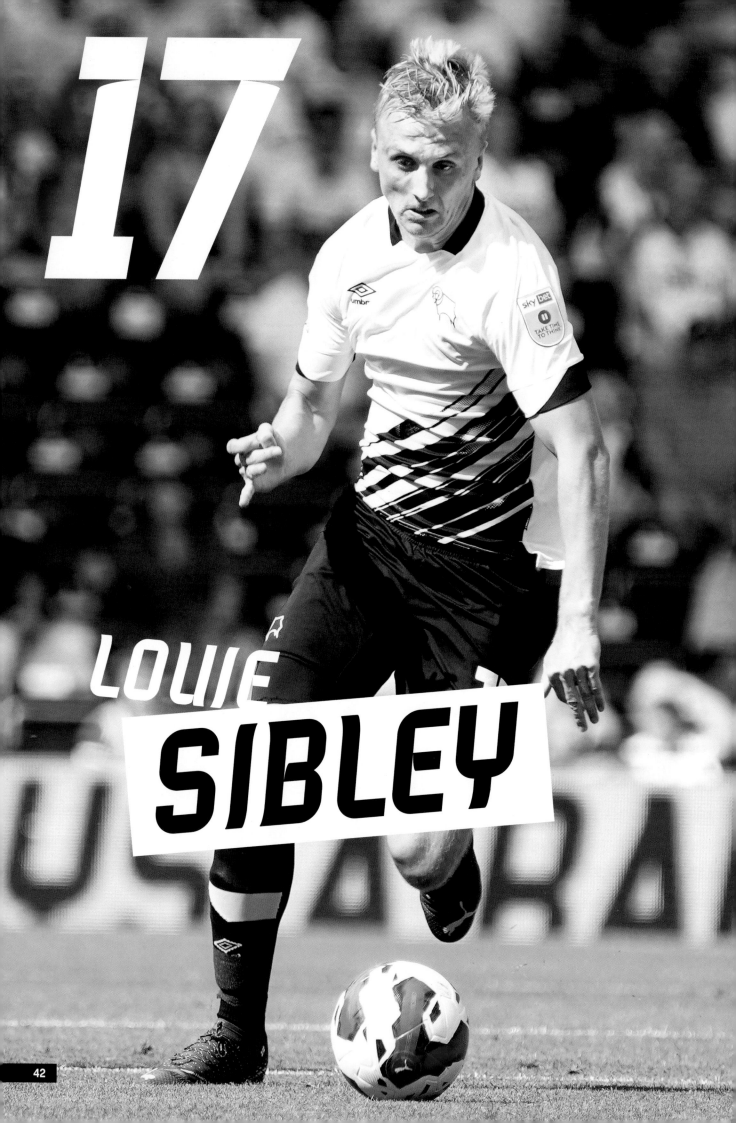

17

LOUIE SIBLEY

TRUE OR FALSE?

ANSWERS ON PAGE 62

Here are ten fun footy True or False teasers for you to tackle! Good luck...

1. England star Harry Kane has only ever played club football for Spurs

2. The FIFA World Cup in 2026 is due to be hosted in the USA, Mexico and Canada

3. Manchester City's former ground was called Maine Park

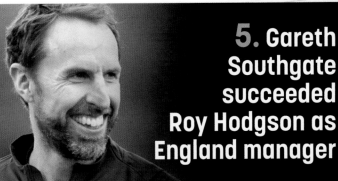

4. Liverpool's Jurgen Klopp has never managed the German national team

5. Gareth Southgate succeeded Roy Hodgson as England manager

6. Manchester United's Old Trafford has the largest capacity in the Premier League

7. Jordan Pickford began his career at Everton

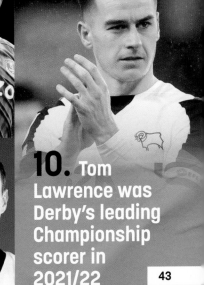

8. Huddersfield Town's nickname is the Terriers

9. Current Rams defender James Chester is a full Republic of Ireland international

10. Tom Lawrence was Derby's leading Championship scorer in 2021/22

43

NUMBER OF SEASONS WITH THE RAMS:

5

DERBY COUNTY LEAGUE APPEARANCES:

100

DERBY COUNTY LEAGUE GOALS:

7

PLAYER OF THE SEASON WINNER:

2000/01

LEGEND

CHRIS RIGGOTT

HONOURS:

Football League Cup winners with Middlesbrough in 2003/04

UEFA Cup finalist with Middlesbrough in 2005/06

MAJOR STRENGTH:

An aerial threat, Riggott would head clear of his own box, and was a threat in the opposition's box too

INTERNATIONAL ACTION:

Riggott made nine appearances for the England U21s at the turn of the millenium

FINEST HOUR:

Playing his final match for Derby County - his 100th for the club whose academy he'd graduated through

Chris Riggott was a local lad who spent two spells at Derby County.

Horacio Carbonari was anything but local, joining the Rams in 1998 from Rosario Central in Argentina. He became the first Argentine ever to play in the Premier League (along with Sheffield Wednesday's Juan Cobián).

Two goalscoring centre-backs, but which is more of a Derby County club legend?

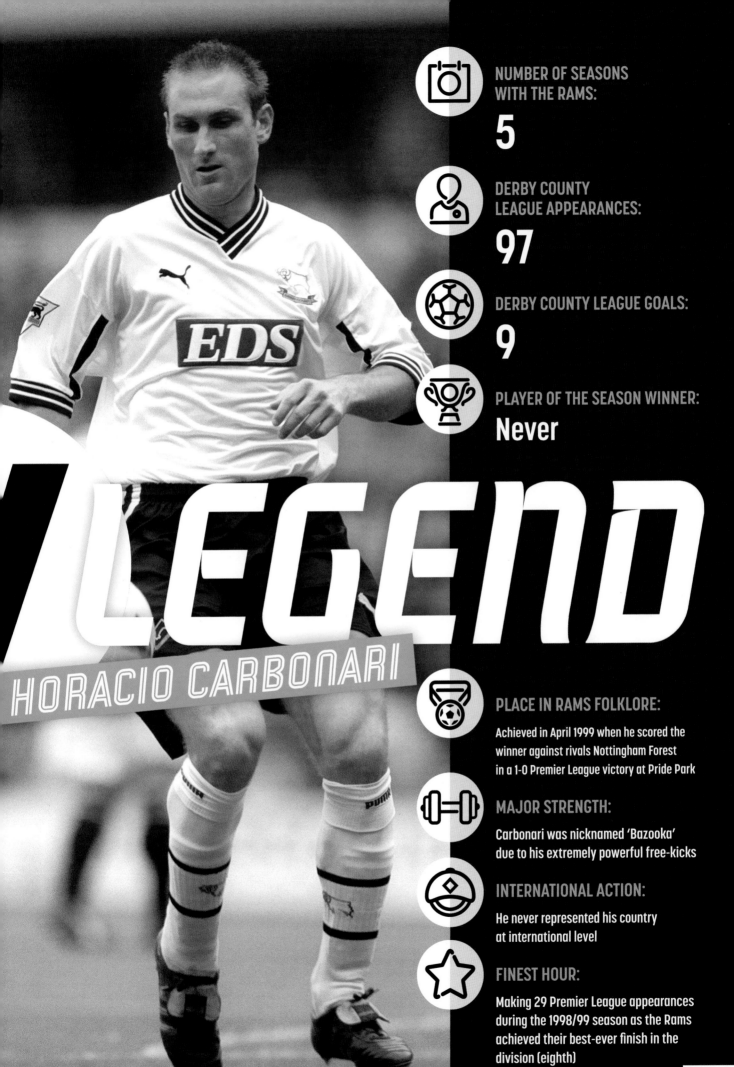

NUMBER OF SEASONS
WITH THE RAMS:

5

DERBY COUNTY
LEAGUE APPEARANCES:

97

DERBY COUNTY LEAGUE GOALS:

9

PLAYER OF THE SEASON WINNER:

Never

LEGEND

HORACIO CARBONARI

PLACE IN RAMS FOLKLORE:

Achieved in April 1999 when he scored the
winner against rivals Nottingham Forest
in a 1-0 Premier League victory at Pride Park

MAJOR STRENGTH:

Carbonari was nicknamed 'Bazooka'
due to his extremely powerful free-kicks

INTERNATIONAL ACTION:

He never represented his country
at international level

FINEST HOUR:

Making 29 Premier League appearances
during the 1998/99 season as the Rams
achieved their best-ever finish in the
division (eighth)

CLUB SEARCH

EVERY TEAM IN LEAGUE ONE IS HIDDEN IN THE GRID, EXCEPT FOR ONE... CAN YOU WORK OUT WHICH ONE?

```
M I L T O N K E Y N E S D O N S O B G S
Q J C S M Y E L S N R A B R L E X O W H
A F H H O N W O T H C I W S P I F L S E
G O A R H B F C U K T N I A C C O T R F
E R R E X E T E R C I T Y D H S R O E F
E E L W S N I V Y P H G Z Q E R D N R I
L S T S M O R E C A M B E V L E U W E E
Y T O B H I Y P D N M X A V T V N A D L
G G N U T B S B M J L N I E O I N N D
R R A R U L N L K J E O N P N R T D A W
A E T Y O A U T I G N U O S H L E E W E
H E H T M N O L K M E R H U A O D R E D
T N L O S O C Z W G T P B Y M T S E B N
U R E W T T Y A D V R E P D T S B R M E
O O T N R R B I A Y A F G L O I F S O S
M V I B O U R L X V B A V M W R K D C D
Y E C F P B E N H Q L T C W N B J C Y A
L R P C M O D L I N C O L N C I T Y W Y
P S R A D N W O T D O O W T E E L F P W
A C C R I N G T O N S T A N L E Y S U I
```

Accrington Stanley
Barnsley
Bolton Wanderers
Bristol Rovers
Burton Albion
Cambridge United

Charlton Athletic
Cheltenham Town
Derby County
Exeter City
Fleetwood Town
Forest Green Rovers

Ipswich Town
Lincoln City
Milton Keynes Dons
Morecambe
Oxford United
Peterborough United

Plymouth Argyle
Port Vale
Portsmouth
Sheffield Wednesday
Shrewsbury Town
Wycombe Wanderers

DAVID
McGOLDRICK

10

47

WHICH BALL?

Can you work out which is the actual match ball in these two action pics?

ANSWERS ON PAGE

NAME THE SEASON

ANSWERS ON PAGE 62

Can you recall the campaign when these magic moments occurred?

Good luck...

1. In which season did Chelsea last win the UEFA Champions League?

2. When were Manchester United last Premier League champions?

3. At the end of which season were England crowned World Cup winners?

4. In which season did Aleksandar Mitrovic net 43 Championship goals for Fulham?

5. In which season did Leicester City become Premier League champions?

6. When did Tottenham Hotspur last reach the League Cup final?

7. In which season were Sheffield United last promoted to the Premier League?

8. When did Manchester City win their first Premier League title?

9. During which season did the Rams enjoy an 8-7 penalty shoot-out victory over Manchester United in the League Cup?

10. In which season did Derby defeat West Bromwich Albion in the Championship Play-Off final to win promotion to the Premier League?

49

Derby County Football Club WOMEN

First team coach Sam Griffiths went into the season 2022/23 with a new look, younger side after narrowly missing out on promotion to the FA Women's Championship last season.

The Ewe Rams finished second in the National League Northern Premier Division, and with two of last season's stars, top scorer Ellie Gilliatt and player of the year Sherrie McCue, retiring from football, Griffiths looked to rebuild her squad in the summer, which has a more youthful look than of seasons past.

And that put Griffiths in confident mood for the season ahead, even though she knew the challenges that faced her were slightly different from before - moulding a young side from scratch into a team capable of winning the league.

This season has been about stabilising and rebuilding, with players being promoted from the Development squad and some new faces joining from elsewhere, under the stewardship of Griffiths and long-time captain and Derby County stalwart Hannah Ward.

The Ewe Rams got off to a strong start this season, including a 5-0 over Loughborough Lightning and a 6-1 victory against Boldemere St Michaels, with last year's Young player of the Year Amy Sims - promoted from right-back to further upfield - scoring hat-tricks in both games.

"It's a really exciting season for us" said boss Griffiths. "It's a new kind of challenge with so many young players, but the energy they have brought us has been fantastic.

"Some of them might lack a bit of experience, but they run and run, get on the front foot, move the ball around; it's been great to watch and they will only learn and get better."

With the women's game receiving unprecedented interest following the Lionessess' victory at the 2022 European Championships, bumper crowds have watched the Ewe Rams this season and, the club, which has eleven teams between Under 8 and Under 20, is certainly building for the future.

51

1. WHO AM I?

2. WHO AM I?

3. WHO AM I?

4. WHO AM I?

52

ANSWERS ON PAGE 62

WHO ARE YER?

Can you figure out who each of these Rams stars is?

5.   WHO AM I?

6.   WHO AM I?

7.   WHO AM I?

8.   WHO AM I?

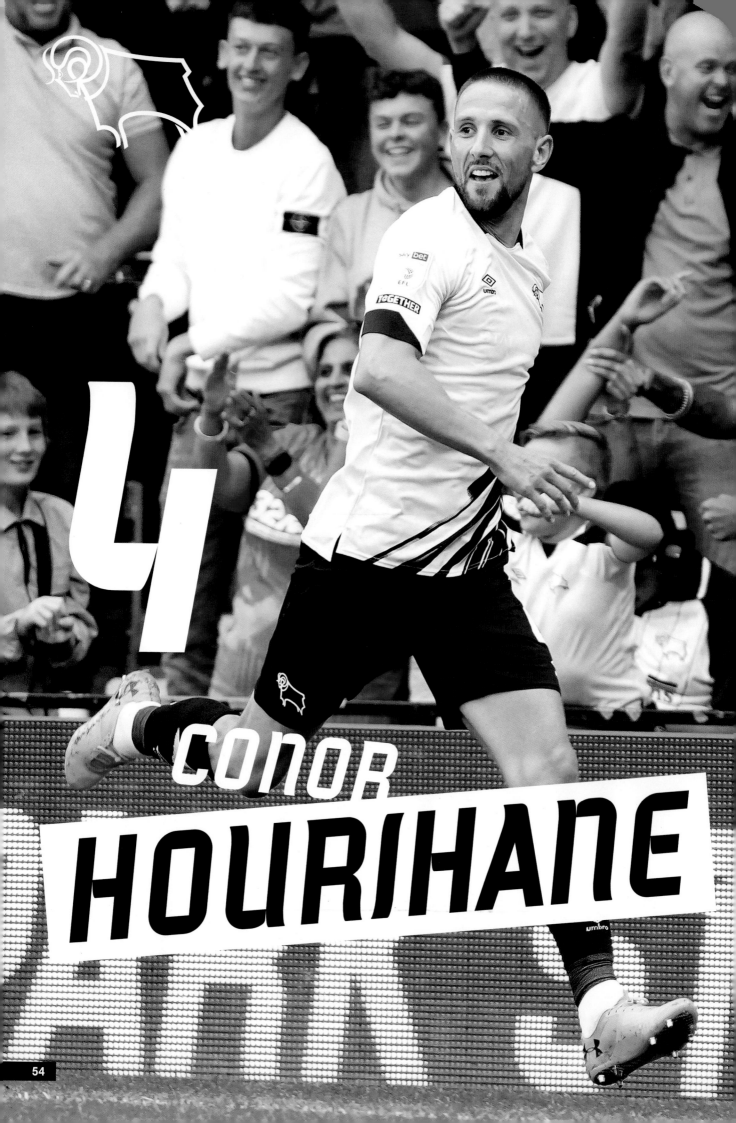

4

CONOR
HOURIHANE

TRUE COLOURS

Can you colour in this picture of Conor Hourihane?

PREMIER LEAGUE CHAMPIONS
Liverpool

FAST FORWARD>>

Do your predictions for 2022/23 match our own?...

CHAMPIONSHIP WINNERS
Millwall

CHAMPIONSHIP

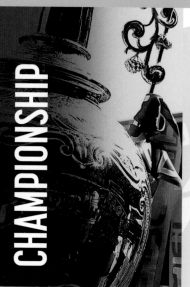

CHAMPIONSHIP RUNNERS-UP
Norwich City

PREMIER LEAGUE

PREMIER LEAGUE RUNNERS-UP
Chelsea

PREMIER LEAGUE TOP SCORER
Erling Haaland

CHAMPIONSHIP TOP SCORER
Michael Obafemi

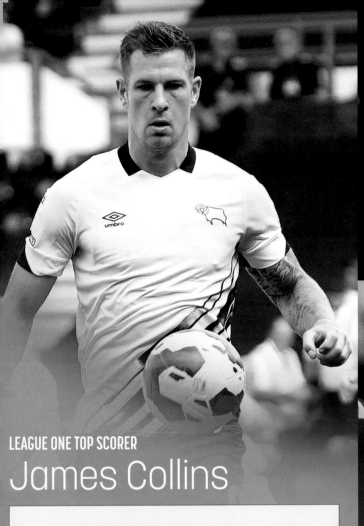

LEAGUE ONE TOP SCORER
James Collins

FA CUP WINNERS
Spurs

LEAGUE CUP WINNERS
Leicester City

LEAGUE CUP

LEAGUE ONE CHAMPIONS
Derby County

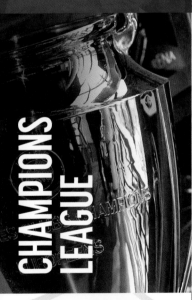

CHAMPIONS LEAGUE

CHAMPIONS LEAGUE WINNERS
Real Madrid

LEAGUE ONE RUNNERS-UP
Oxford United

LEAGUE ONE

EUROPA LEAGUE WINNERS
Roma

EUROPA LEAGUE

NUMBER OF SEASONS WITH THE RAMS:

10

DERBY COUNTY LEAGUE APPEARANCES:

214

DERBY COUNTY LEAGUE GOALS:

59

PLAYER OF THE SEASON WINNER:

Never

LEGEND
DEAN STURRIDGE

DERBY COUNTY ACHIEVEMENTS:

First Division runners-up
1995/96
Anglo-Italian Cup runners-up
1992/93

MAJOR STRENGTH:

Putting the ball in the back
of the net and strong link-up play

INTERNATIONAL ACTION:

Sturridge never represented
his country

FINEST HOUR:

Graduating to the first team,
having been a Derby County
trainee

For Dean Sturridge, Derby County was the striker's first team. For Deon Burton, it was his third.

But in both cases, Derbyshire is where they spent their best years. Between them, the two prolific centre-forwards spent 15 years with the Rams.

But who has the edge as the greatest Derby striker?

NUMBER OF SEASONS WITH THE RAMS:

5

DERBY COUNTY LEAGUE APPEARANCES:

143

DERBY COUNTY LEAGUE GOALS:

31

PLAYER OF THE SEASON WINNER:

Never

LEGEND

DEON BURTON

PLACE IN RAMS FOLKLORE:

Rams Top Goalscorer
1998/99

MAJOR STRENGTH:

Poachers' finishes from close range, usually with his right foot or head

INTERNATIONAL ACTION:

Despite being born in Reading, Burton turned out for Jamaica, and won Jamaican Sportsperson of the Year in 1997 for almost single-handedly getting the Reggae Boyz to the 1998 World Cup. In total, he won 62 caps in a twelve-year international career, notching 13 goals

FINEST HOUR:

For Deon, it was the whole experience. He called his period at Derby 'the most rewarding time' of his career

IDENTIFY THE STAR

Can you put a name to the footy stars in these ten teasers?

Good luck...

ANSWERS ON PAGE 62

1. Manchester City's title-winning 'keeper Ederson shared the 2021/22 Golden Glove award for the number of clean sheets with which Premier League rival?

2. Which Portuguese superstar re-joined Manchester United in the 2021/22 season?

3. Can you name the Brazilian forward who joined Aston Villa in May 2022 following a loan spell at Villa Park?

4. Who became Arsenal manager in 2019?

5. Who scored the winning goal in the 2021/22 UEFA Champions League final?

6. After 550 games for West Ham United, which long-serving midfielder announced his retirement in 2022?

7. Who took the mantle of scoring Brentford's first Premier League goal?

8. Who scored the final goal for Manchester City in their 2021/22 Premier League title-winning season?

9. Who was Derby County manager when the Rams thrashed arch-rivals Nottingham Forest 5-0 at Pride Park in March 2014?

10. Can you name the Derby player who scored the final goal of his career in the Rams' 1-0 victory at Norwich City in October 2020?

60

9

JAMES COLLINS

ANSWERS

PAGE 26 · MULTIPLE CHOICE

1. C. 2. B. 3. A. 4. B. 5. C. 6. A. 7. B. 8. B. 9. A. 10. C.

PAGE 28 · FAN'TASTIC

PAGE 43 · TRUE OR FALSE?

1. False, Harry played on loan for Leyton Orient, Millwall, Norwich City & Leicester City. 2. True. 3. False, it was called Maine Road. 4. True. 5. False, Gareth succeeded Sam Allardyce. 6. True. 7. False, Jordan began his career at Sunderland. 8. True. 9. False, he is a Wales international. 10. True.

PAGE 46 · CLUB SEARCH

Peterborough United

PAGE 48 · WHICH BALL?

PAGE 49 · NAME THE SEASON

1. 2020/21. 2. 2012/13. 3. 1965/66. 4. 2021/22. 5. 2015/16. 6. 2020/21. 7. 2018/19. 8. 2011/12. 9. 2018/19. 10. 2006/07.

PAGE 52 · WHO ARE YER?

1. Conor Hourihane. 2. David McGoldrick. 3. Curtis Davies. 4. Lewis Dobbin. 5. Richard Stearman. 6. Jason Knight. 7. Tom Barkuizen. 8. Korey Smith.

PAGE 60 · IDENTIFY THE STAR

1. Allison Becker (Liverpool). 2. Cristiano Ronaldo. 3. Philippe Coutinho. 4. Mikel Arteta. 5. Vinícius Júnior. 6. Mark Noble. 7. Sergi Canós. 8. İlkay Gündoğan. 9. Steve McClaren. 10. Wayne Rooney.